## Date Due

# CATERPILLARS
## AND HOW THEY LIVE

WRITTEN AND ILLUSTRATED BY
## ROBERT M. McCLUNG

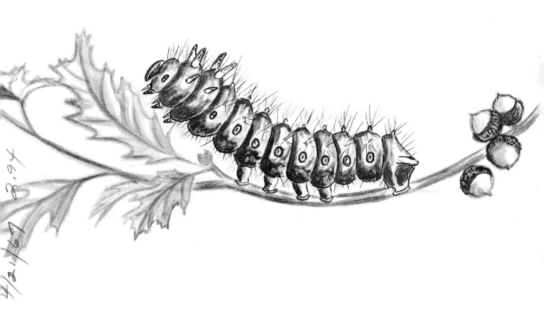

WILLIAM MORROW AND COMPANY
NEW YORK 1965

Grateful recognition is given to
Dr. Lincoln P. Brower,
Associate Professor of Biology,
Amherst College,
for reading and criticizing the manuscript.

Published simultaneously in the Dominion of Canada
by George P. McLeod Limited, Toronto.
Printed in the United States of America.
Library of Congress Catalog Card Number 65-20949

. . .

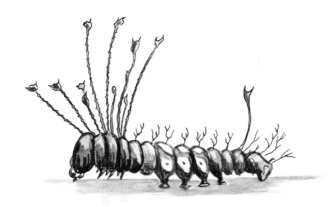

# CONTENTS

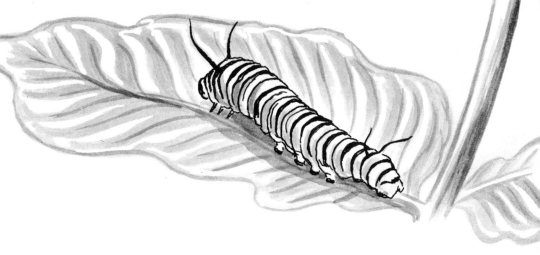

## ONE          WHAT IS A CATERPILLAR?

Summer and early fall are the best times to look for caterpillars. Then you may see them wherever you go—if you use your eyes.

Perhaps a little worm swings from a silken thread, right in front of your nose. Or an inch-worm humps its way across your sleeve. You pretend that it is measuring you for a new jacket.

Maybe you see a brightly colored caterpillar on a milkweed plant. Its black and yellow stripes remind you of a tiger. A woolly bear caterpillar crosses the path in front of you. You touch it and it curls up into a fuzzy ball, like a little black-and-brown pincushion.

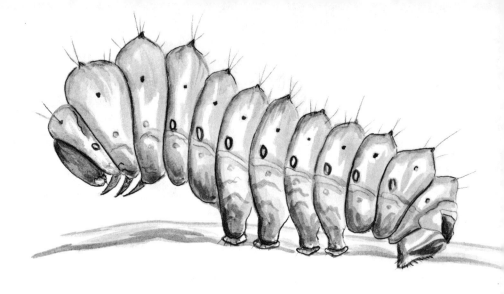

One day you see a big green caterpillar crawling down a tree trunk. Here is a giant of the tribe— one of our native American silkworms. Let it crawl onto your finger. It won't bite or hurt you. Its feet may feel a little ticklish or prickly—that is all. Now take a good look at it.

### The Segmented Body

The plump body is long and wormlike, and has a row of spots along each side. They are spiracles— openings through which the caterpillar breathes. Each spiracle connects with a branching air tube inside the body.

The body itself is divided into thirteen distinct rings or segments. On each of the first three are a pair of short, clawlike legs. The caterpillar grasps a leaf with these legs when it eats. But it can't walk with them.

The caterpillar walks on five pairs of fleshy limbs, or claspers— four pairs in the middle of its body and a pair at the very end. They are called prolegs. The caterpillar will eventually lose them.

Each proleg ends in a flat sole that clasps onto a surface like a vacuum cup. The sole is bordered with many tiny hooklets, or claws, which help the caterpillar to hold on. They cause the prickly feeling on your finger.

Watch the way the prolegs move ahead in succession as the caterpillar crawls. It is using hundreds of tiny muscles. You have nearly 800 muscles in your body, which seem like a lot. But a caterpillar has at least twice that many.

*The Jaws and Face*

Now look at the caterpillar's head and watch how it eats a leaf. With a magnifying glass you can easily see how the two hinged jaws work. They have toothed inner edges and move sideways against each other like a pair of scissors.

Just above the jaws is a little notched plate—the caterpillar's upper lip. The lower lip is on the underside of the head, behind the jaws. A little tube, or nozzle, sticks out of the center of it. It is the spinneret, the opening for the caterpillar's silk glands.

To either side of the spinneret are two tiny palps, or feelers. On beyond them are larger structures called antennae, one on either side of the face. The

8

antennae and palps are sense organs. The caterpillar feels with them and, perhaps, smells with
them too.

The caterpillar can't see very well. Its eyes are
two half circles of tiny dots. These simple eyes can
tell light from darkness and possibly make out
simple objects like leaves or twigs. But they probably can't see anything more than a few inches
away. The caterpillar depends mostly on its sense
of touch.

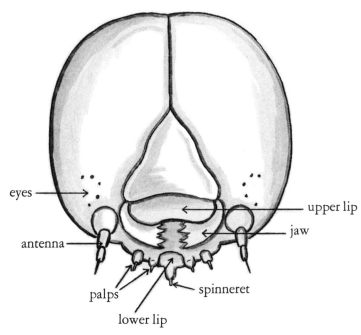

HEAD OF A CATERPILLAR

*Many Kinds*

No matter what it looks like, every caterpillar has much the same type of head and body. Some caterpillars—the big family of measuring worms, or inchworms—have only two pairs of prolegs. They are located at the rear end of the body. A measuring worm walks by stretching forward, then humping its body into a loop as it draws its rear end up. Stretch and hump, stretch and hump. That's the way a measuring worm crawls about.

Measuring worms are long and thin, but various other caterpillars may be short and thick, or flat and stubby. Some caterpillars have smooth naked bodies, while others have dense coats of woolly hair or bristly spines. Some are decorated all over with knobs, or warts. Still others have long curved horns.

prominent moth

tiger swallowtail

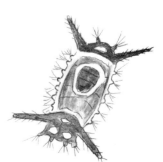

saddleback

woolly bear
(Isabella tiger moth)

pipevine swallowtail

white-marked tussock moth

SOME DIFFERENT
CATERPILLARS

white flannel
moth

hag moth

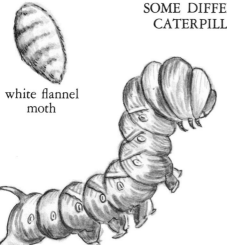

tomato hornworm
(sphinx moth)

milkweed tussock moth

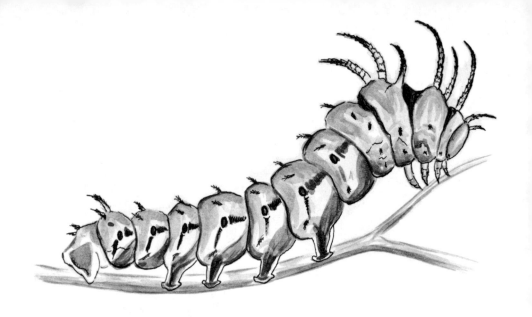

One of the biggest of all caterpillars is called the hickory horned devil. About six inches long when full grown, it is brightly striped and has many fearsome-looking horns. In spite of its frightening appearance, it is really quite harmless.

Big or little, bare or fuzzy, all caterpillars have the same general body plan, the same basic structures. Examine any number of them closely, and you will see that this is true.

Many people call caterpillars *worms*. But this name is not correct. A true worm, such as the earthworm, remains a worm throughout its entire life.

It is not an insect. But a caterpillar is an immature, or larval, insect. If it lives, it will eventually become a butterfly or a moth. Before this happens, however, it must go through an inactive, or pupal, stage. Wonderful changes take place inside the pupa.

If you collect some caterpillars and keep them, you will discover these things for yourself. Perhaps you will be lucky enough to find a big green Cecropia caterpillar, just like the one pictured below. It is fairly common, and you may find it on a tree in your backyard.

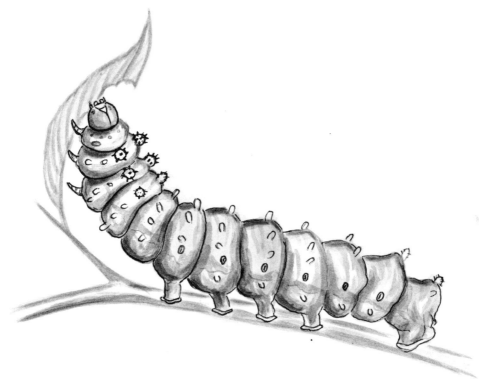

If you do find one, keep it and feed it. Watch it spin its cocoon. Eventually a big Cecropia moth will hatch from that cocoon. It will look as big as a bird.

If you let her go, the female Cecropia moth will mate and lay many eggs. They will be the start of a new generation of caterpillars.

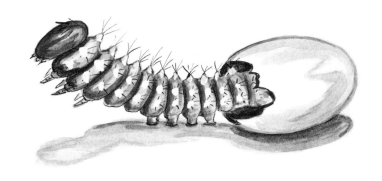

## TWO        THE LIFE OF THE CATERPILLAR

The Cecropia moth lays her eggs on leaves, cementing them in place with a sticky liquid that quickly dries. Each egg is mostly white and has a smooth tough shell. It looks something like a chicken egg, but is very much smaller. A dozen Cecropia eggs laid end to end would measure only an inch.

Tiny Cecropia caterpillars hatch from the eggs in about ten days. They are blackish and are covered with many branching spines. When full grown, they will become huge green caterpillars.

| monarch butterfly | fall cankerworm | silver-spotted skipper | spring azure butterfly | Baltimore butterfly |

BUTTERFLY AND MOTH EGGS

Every caterpillar starts life as an egg. Some of the eggs are so tiny that you can hardly see them with your naked eye. Even the largest are no bigger than tiny beads.

*All Sorts of Eggs*

Some moth and butterfly eggs are oval, while others are perfectly round. Still others may be shaped like little barrels or cones or flat discs. Some even look like little sausages. Many have smooth shells, while others are ribbed or sculptured in fancy designs. They may be white or green or yellow—or any color you can imagine.

Each female moth or butterfly usually lays several hundred eggs, but the number varies. Most of them

purslane
moth

Polyphemus
moth

clouded sulphur
butterfly

common blue
butterfly

painted lady
butterfly

deposit each of their many eggs in a different place. Some, however, lay them all together in clusters. Eggs laid in the spring or summer usually hatch within a few days. But those laid in the fall may not hatch until the following spring.

No matter how or when they are laid, the eggs are always placed where there will be a good supply of the right kind of food for the caterpillars as soon as they hatch. Many caterpillars eat only one particular food and refuse everything else.

Caterpillars of the monarch butterfly eat only milkweed leaves. Caterpillars of the black swallowtail eat only leaves of carrots and related plants. The females of these butterflies almost always lay their eggs on the right food plants.

The first meal of a newly hatched caterpillar may be its own eggshell. When that is gone, it starts on its regular food.

## Eating and Growing

The great majority of caterpillars are vegetarians. Most of them eat leaves, but some fill up on fruit or seeds—or even wood. Clothes-moth caterpillars dine on wool. And a few others are meat eaters.

The caterpillar of the harvester butterfly eats woolly aphids, a kind of plant lice. And some caterpillars, like those of certain small blue butterflies, are even cannibals. At times they eat their own kind.

Whatever food the caterpillar eats must last it through the pupal stage, and often throughout its winged adult life as well. Butterflies usually sip nectar, but many moths do not eat anything at all. Neither butterflies nor moths need as much nourishment as caterpillars do, however. Adult insects, they do not grow any more.

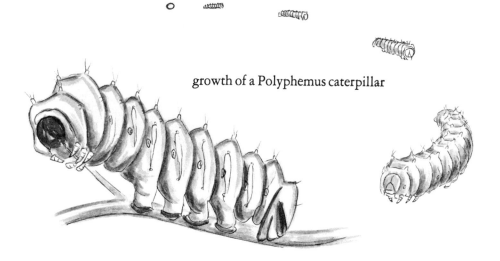

growth of a Polyphemus caterpillar

But caterpillars eat and eat, for they must grow and grow and grow. A scientist once figured that a caterpillar of the Polyphemus moth increased its weight more than 4000 times in 56 days. That takes a lot of eating and growing!

The caterpillar's skin does not grow with it. After a few days of eating the skin becomes tight, just like a suit of clothes that is too small. Then the caterpillar must shed its skin. It finds a good spot and waits quietly. Sometimes it spins a little platform of silk as a resting place.

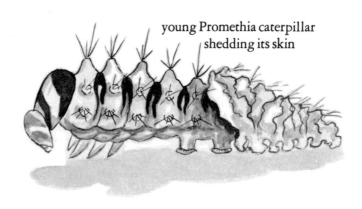

young Promethia caterpillar shedding its skin

*Shedding the Skin*

Soon a tear or rip appears along the caterpillar's back, just behind the head. It slowly becomes longer and longer. Wriggling and twisting, the caterpillar crawls out of its skin, leaving it behind like a crumpled heap of old clothes. At the same time, the hard outer shell of the head falls off. Now the caterpillar is dressed in a completely new and larger skin that has developed under the old one. Once again it has room to grow.

After another few days of eating, the new skin in its turn becomes too tight. The caterpillar then sheds it in the same way. Most caterpillars shed their skins four to six times before they are full grown. Often each new skin looks quite different from the one before it.

Since the caterpillar's main activity is eating, much of the space inside its body is taken up by the gut, or digestive tract. There the food is digested. A lot of it is then stored in fat cells.

On either side of the gut lie the two long silk glands. And above the gut lies the heart—an open tube with slits in its sides. Blood enters the heart through the slits and is pumped out through the open end. It isn't carried in veins and arteries as our

INSIDE A CATERPILLAR

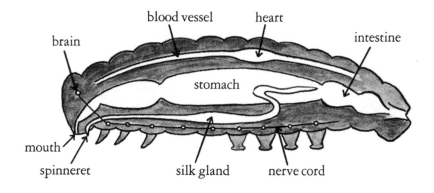

brain · blood vessel · heart · intestine · stomach · mouth · spinneret · silk gland · nerve cord

blood is, but flows freely through the body cavity. The blood isn't red like our blood, either. It may be pale green or yellow, or it may be colorless.

*Where They Live*

Most of the caterpillars you find will usually be out in the open, crawling about on some tree or plant. But not all of them live this way. Many of them keep out of sight much of the time.

The corn borer conceals itself inside stalks or ears of corn. Wood-boring caterpillars tunnel inside tree trunks or limbs. The caterpillar of the carpenter moth may live in a tree trunk for two years or more before it pupates. It eats wood pulp.

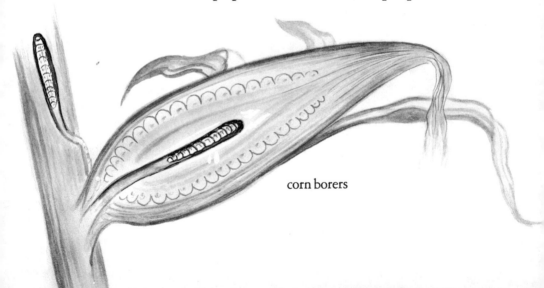

corn borers

Some very tiny caterpillars called leaf miners, or borers, live *inside* leaves. They tunnel through the thin layer of cells that lies between the upper and lower surfaces of the leaf.

Lots of caterpillars live inside fruit or seeds. The caterpillar of the Oriental fruit moth is the little white worm you sometimes find when you bite into a peach. And Mexican jumping beans are beans that have tiny caterpillars living inside them. When the caterpillar wriggles, the bean jumps.

Cutworms conceal themselves in little burrows, which they dig in the ground. They hide in them all day long. But at night they come out to gnaw on plant stalks and garden seedlings.

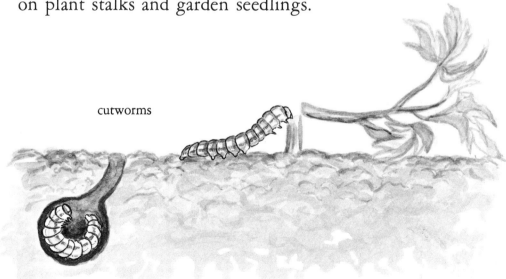

cutworms

A few caterpillars live inside growths or swellings on plants. These growths are called galls. They are usually formed as a result of chemicals given off by some insect. Many kinds of insects besides caterpillars cause galls.

The caterpillar of one tiny moth lives inside a gall that is commonly formed on stalks of goldenrod. Before it pupates, the little caterpillar tunnels to the outside of the gall and prepares a round door with a silken lid. Then it pupates on a silk hammock inside. When the moth hatches, it simply pushes out the lid of its escape door and flies away.

goldenrod gall with
caterpillar and moth

lily-leaf caterpillar
and case

A few kinds of caterpillars live in the water and feed on aquatic plants. Some of them build little houses from pieces of lily pad. Several of these aquatic caterpillars breathe through threadlike gills along their sides. Others keep a bubble of air trapped in a leaf hut. They breathe through spiracles, just as most other caterpillars do.

## Colonies

The great majority of caterpillars live alone and do not pay any attention to other caterpillars they may meet. Caterpillars of the same kind sometimes cluster together when they are small. But as they grow and need more food, they usually scatter.

full-grown tent caterpillar and cocoon

A few kinds of caterpillars, however, remain together throughout their whole caterpillar life. Tent caterpillars are familiar examples. They spin silk shelters that are common sights on wild cherry and other trees in springtime.

Tent caterpillars hatch from clusters of eggs laid the summer before by little brown moths. After depositing her eggs in neat rows around a twig, each moth covers them with a frothy liquid that hardens into a tough varnished shell.

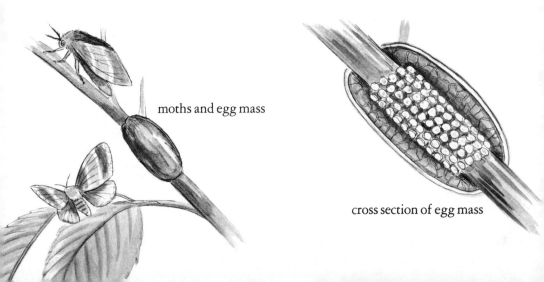

moths and egg mass

cross section of egg mass

eggs (enlarged)

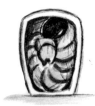

caterpillar curled up in egg

Tiny caterpillars develop within the eggs after several weeks. But they don't hatch then. They remain curled snugly within their shells all winter long.

But when springtime comes and leaves begin to sprout, the eggs hatch. Each little caterpillar cuts a round opening in the top of the egg with its jaws. Crawling out, it huddles on the twig with its newly hatched brothers and sisters. Soon the caterpillars spin a little silk tent for a community shelter. They

newly hatched caterpillars

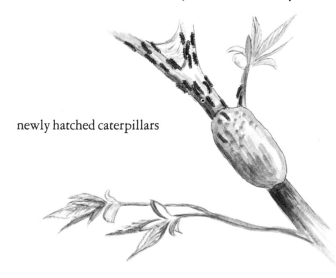

leave it only at mealtime. Whenever it leaves the
nest, each caterpillar spins a silk thread as a glistening trail behind it. Finished eating, the caterpillar
follows the trail of silk back home.

As the caterpillars grow, they make their tent larger and larger. The colony does not break up until the caterpillars are ready to spin cocoons.

Many years ago the famous French naturalist, Jean Henri Fabre, conducted a series of experiments with pine processionary caterpillars. They live in colonies and spin webs as tent caterpillars do. Fabre noticed that the caterpillars always filed out of the nest in a line, each one following the silken trail laid down by the caterpillar in front of it.

One day he watched a file of caterpillars crawl up the side of a large wooden plant tub. The leader started around the rim and the others followed. When the rim was crowded with a complete circle of caterpillars, Fabre broke the silken trail that led to the rim and removed it. He watched to see what the caterpillars would do.

Round and round the rim they went, each one blindly following the caterpillar ahead, each one adding its silk to the circular trail. None would venture away from the path, which had always before led them back to their nest.

They circled the rim for nearly eight days. In all that time they had nothing to eat, although plenty of their food was located only a few inches from the tub. On the third day one venturesome group did break away to crawl up the palm in the center of the tub. But soon the explorers crawled down and, once again, took up their position on the rim.

At last one famished individual blazed a new trail down the outside of the tub, and the others followed. Finally they were back in familiar territory. But the caterpillars hadn't shown the faintest glimmer of sense during their eight-day march. They survived only because of a lucky chance.

## THREE        THE STRUGGLE FOR SURVIVAL

Caterpillars are always in danger of being eaten by one kind of animal or another. Birds gobble down great numbers of them. A single pair of birds may gather hundreds of caterpillars daily to feed to their hungry nestlings.

Mice and chipmunks and many other mammals eat caterpillars too. So do frogs and toads, lizards, snakes, and fish. Even other insects, such as stink-bugs, often prey on caterpillars.

stinkbug attacking young luna caterpillar

Stinkbugs have long sharp beaks like hypodermic needles. They thrust them into caterpillars and paralyze their victims with injections of poisonous saliva. Then they suck out the juices, leaving the caterpillars empty shells.

One day you may find a caterpillar with a lot of tiny white cocoons on its back. They are cocoons spun by the larvae of a little wasp. The wasp laid her eggs on the caterpillar some days before you found it. When they hatched, the wasp larvae burrowed inside the caterpillar's body and fed on it.

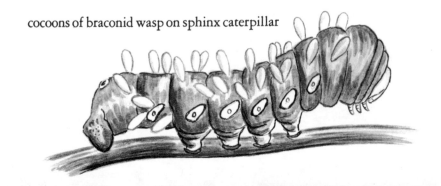

cocoons of braconid wasp on sphinx caterpillar

ichneumon wasp
laying egg on
Polyphemus caterpillar

Full grown, they tunneled out and spun their co-coons. The caterpillar soon dies.

The larvae of various flies also feed on caterpillars, and so do the young of certain ichneumon wasps. Some ichneumons pierce the caterpillar's skin with what looks like a long spear at the end of the body. This is the egg-laying organ.

The potter wasp preys on caterpillars in another way. It first builds a neat little clay jug on a twig. Then it stocks the jug with caterpillars, which it has paralyzed with its sting. Finally it lays an egg

potter wasp and its clay nest

in the jug and seals the opening. When the wasp larva hatches, it has a plentiful supply of fresh caterpillar meat for its food.

*Shelters*

Caterpillars protect themselves in many ways against their host of enemies. Some of them build individual shelters or hiding places. The hiding place may be a leaf, which the caterpillar merely folds or bends over and fastens in place with silk. Or it may be a small section of a leaf rolled into a hollow tube and bound in the same way. The caterpillar of the viceroy butterfly remains snug in such a rolled leaf hut all winter long.

silver-spotted skipper

Caterpillars of skippers, swift little butterflies with light-spotted brown wings, fasten two or more locust leaves together to make shelters.

The bagworm spins a tough silken case, the outside of which is decorated with bits of leaves or sticks. The caterpillar enlarges the bag as it grows and carries it about wherever it travels. Finally it pupates inside the shelter.

The female moth is wingless and never leaves the bag after she hatches. She mates with the winged male through an opening in the end of her case. Soon afterward she dies. When tiny bagworms hatch from her eggs, they venture forth and build cases of their own.

bagworm

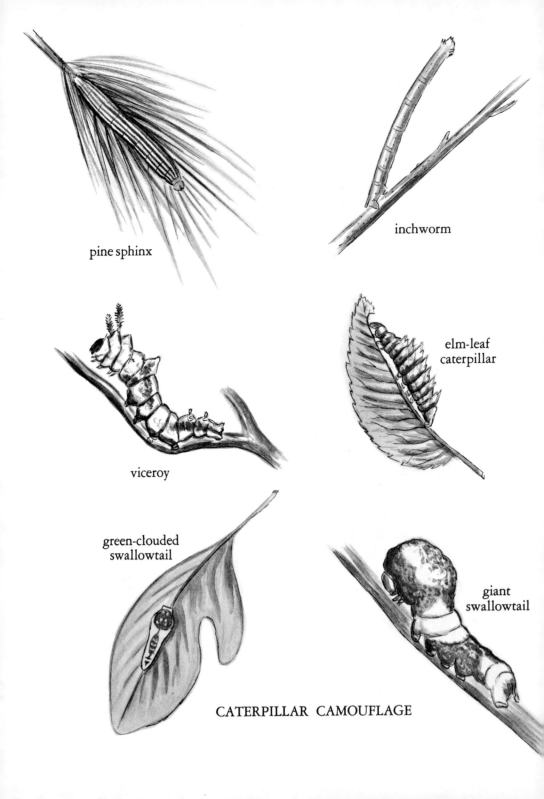

pine sphinx

inchworm

elm-leaf
caterpillar

viceroy

green-clouded
swallowtail

giant
swallowtail

CATERPILLAR CAMOUFLAGE

*Camouflage*

Caterpillars that don't build shelters are often protected by their concealing color or shape. Many are the same shade of green as the leaves they eat. Some have spots or stripes that resemble tiny holes in the leaves, or leaf veins. The pine sphinx caterpillar has an overall pattern of long narrow stripes that run from one end of its body to the other. It is almost invisible among the pine needles it eats.

Other caterpillars are mostly brown or gray, and look like dead or withered leaves. Huge humps or horns often add to the resemblance.

Inchworms often imitate twigs. Hanging onto a branch by its rear prolegs, an inchworm thrusts the rest of its body stiffly outward. As long as it remains motionless, it looks like part of the plant.

Still other caterpillars have large areas of contrasting light and dark colors that tend to conceal their general outline and make them look like something else. Young caterpillars of some swallowtail

butterflies are marked in this fashion with gray and white. Resting motionless on leaves, they look very much like bird droppings.

*Warding Off Enemies*

The queer little puss-moth caterpillar is mostly green, but has a big dark saddle on its back. This conceals its body outline by breaking it up into three parts. If it is disturbed, the puss-moth caterpillar brings other defenses into play. Thrusting its head and rear end into the air, it lashes two long tails about. They resemble weapons, but are harmless.

Many caterpillars drop to the ground if they are attacked. Various others curl into tight balls.

The caterpillars of hawk moths rear their bodies into the air in a threatening manner. Sometimes they twist violently from side to side and click their jaws. They look quite fierce.

The monarch caterpillar wears a suit of gay yellow and black stripes. This vivid pattern draws attention to the caterpillar and actually helps to protect it by warning birds and other enemies to keep away. This caterpillar tastes bad, probably because of its milkweed-leaf diet. Once a bird tries one, it usually doesn't try another. The caterpillar's bright colors advertise the fact that it isn't good to eat.

Various swallowtail caterpillars have swollen bodies with two big spots on the back that look

green-clouded swallowtail

like eyes. When such a caterpillar rears up, it looks something like the head of a small green snake. Perhaps this resemblance scares away some enemies.

*Weapons for Defense*

But if this defense doesn't work, the swallowtail caterpillar has another. From a slit behind the head it suddenly thrusts out orange, yellow, or red horns. They give off a disagreeable odor that discourages many enemies. Once the danger is gone, the caterpillar pulls the horns back into its body.

A few caterpillars—the red-humped apple worm and some of its relatives—defend themselves by giving off an acid from a gland located behind the

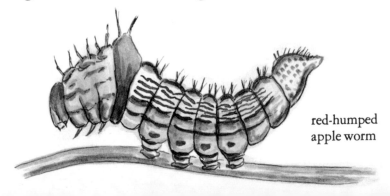

red-humped
apple worm

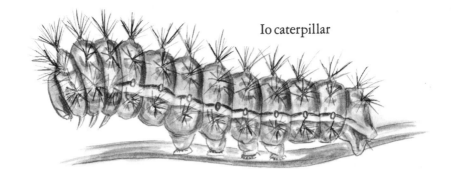

Io caterpillar

head. Some of them can squirt this stinging spray several inches. These acid-producing caterpillars are usually boldly marked with bright warning colors.

Others, such as the Io caterpillar, have bodies that bristle with tufts of sharp poisonous spines. Handle these caterpillars carefully, and don't touch their spines. The poison from them stings and itches and often raises welts on your skin.

Many caterpillars like the woolly bear are protected by their thick coats of hair or bristles. These hairs are not poisonous, but they protect the caterpillar anyway. Rolled up, a woolly bear is a difficult mouthful for a bird to eat. Swallowing one would be like eating a tiny, curled-up porcupine!

woolly bear

*Protected by Ants*

Some caterpillars—those of the blue butterflies, for example—give off a sweet liquid called honeydew from openings on their backs. Ants are very fond of honeydew and greedily lap it up from the caterpillars' bodies. In return, the ants protect the caterpillars from insect enemies.

A scientist recently discovered one such caterpillar in Mexico. It is kept by ants in much the same way that we keep dairy cows. Watching, he noted that the ants herded their honeydew "cattle" into their underground nests every night for safekeeping. Every morning they escorted the caterpillars back onto their food bushes, like putting cows out to pasture. Acting as shepherds, the ants guarded the caterpillars all day long and came to their defense whenever anything threatened them.

## FOUR          CATERPILLARS AND MAN

There are a few kinds of caterpillars that often do great damage to trees or crops. They sometimes appear in countless hordes that destroy entire grainfields or ruin most of the fruit harvest throughout a whole region.

The caterpillar of the coddling moth is one of the pests that spoils fruit. It is the little worm that you sometimes find when you are eating an apple. Different caterpillars destroy other fruits and vegetables in much the same way.

In the garden, cutworms nip through the stalks of newly planted tomato plants and destroy seedling vegetables. Caterpillars of a little white butterfly eat cabbage leaves. Big tomato hornworms sometimes strip entire tomato plants of their leaves.

The clothes moth even invades our homes and lays its eggs on stored woolens. The tiny caterpillars eat the wool and make holes in the cloth. That's why many carpets and other woolen materials are treated with chemicals today to make them moth-proof. That's why your mother puts mothballs or naphtha flakes in with woolen clothes when she stores them away for the summer.

One of the worst grain pests is the corn borer, the caterpillar of a small brown European moth. It bores through stalks or ears of corn. Corn borers were brought to the United States fifty or more years ago, hidden in broomcorn—a kind of corn used in making brooms.

Another harmful immigrant is the gypsy moth. It came to America in 1869, introduced by a man who hoped to use the caterpillar in starting a silk industry in Massachusetts. Some of his caterpillars escaped. Quickly adapting to the new country, the gypsy moth spread throughout the Northeast. Now the caterpillars sometimes appear in great hordes that strip most of the leaves from entire forests.

*Controlling Pests*

Outbreaks of such pests are usually combatted with poisons called insecticides. They are often sprayed from airplanes. Insecticides help to control the pests, but they frequently kill useful insects, birds, and other animals as well. They can be very dangerous to man, too.

male gypsy moths
flying to trap

Because of this problem, scientists are now searching for new ways of fighting harmful insects. Ideal methods are those that will control the pests without harming other life. Encouraging such natural enemies as birds or parasitic wasps helps. So does the use of bacterial or fungus diseases that attack particular pests, but will not affect other animals.

Moth traps are sometimes used to help control the gypsy moth. These traps use scent obtained from female gypsy moths as bait to attract and capture great numbers of male moths in an area. As a result, many of the female gypsy moths cannot find mates. They lay infertile eggs that do not hatch.

## Some Are Useful

Most kinds of caterpillars do not occur in such numbers that they ever do much harm. A few kinds are even useful to man. Primitive tribes in some parts of Africa, Australia, and tropical America gather caterpillars for food. They dry them or roast them or sometimes eat them raw—and consider them very tasty.

The caterpillar of a certain South American moth helps to control cactus. Many years ago the prickly pear cactus was introduced into Australia. There it spread quickly. By 1925 it had invaded sixty million or more acres, making much of the area useless for crops. Many methods for controlling the cactus were tried, but with little success. Then eggs of the South American cactus moth were brought in. The caterpillars of this moth bore through cactus leaves and stems and open the way for diseases that kill the cactus. Within fifteen years these caterpillars had brought the cactus under control.

### The Silkworm

Of all useful caterpillars, the best known is the domestic silkworm. For thousands of years the Chinese have raised silkworms on mulberry leaves and woven their silk into soft, shimmering fabrics. For many centuries the Chinese guarded the secrets of silk culture jealously. But other Asiatic countries eventually learned the methods and started their own silk industries.

It was not until the sixth century, however, that Western countries discovered these secrets and started to raise silkworms. One story is that two monks hid silkworm eggs and mulberry seeds in a hollow cane and smuggled them back to Constantinople about the year 550.

Gradually silk culture became an important industry in Italy, France, and other European countries. It has been tried in the United States too, but with little success—mostly because of labor costs.

Each female silk moth lays 300 or 400 eggs, which hatch in about a week's time. The caterpillars are kept in huge flat trays and fed fresh mulberry leaves. Full grown, they are about three inches long. Then they spin glistening white cocoons.

The cocoons are gathered and sorted by size. Next they are boiled to kill the pupae and to soften the silk fibers. An experienced worker finds and separates the end of the silken thread of each cocoon. Five to seven of these threads are twisted together. This stronger and thicker fiber is attached to a spindle, which unwinds the silk from the cocoons. The silk is then woven into cloth.

Each silk-moth cocoon is spun from a continuous silken thread that is a half to three quarters of a mile long. Two or three thousand cocoons are needed to make one pound of silk fiber. No wonder silk is an expensive fabric!

Many years ago a big Asiatic moth, the Cynthia, was introduced into the United States with the hope that its silk could be raised commercially. This plan soon failed, and the project was abandoned. But the Cynthia moth established itself in various places where its caterpillar's food plant, the ailanthus, or tree of heaven, grows. The tree flourishes in vacant lots and along roadsides in New York City and many other eastern areas. The beautiful moth has a wingspread of five or six inches.

## FIVE          RAISING CATERPILLARS

You can learn many things about caterpillars by watching them out of doors. Soon you will be able to recognize various kinds and know them as friends.

But if you want to follow a particular caterpillar through its complete life history, you must usually collect it and keep it at home.

It takes practice to become an expert caterpillar hunter. You can find some kinds by searching for half-eaten foliage and looking among it for the caterpillars that ate the leaves. They are often close by. Or you may find caterpillar droppings on a sidewalk or road under trees. Then, if you look carefully, you can often spot the caterpillar on the branch above. Such caterpillars as the monarch can be found by searching for them on their particular food plants.

## Cages and Care

Once you have found them, you can keep the caterpillars in almost any kind of cage. A shoebox with a mosquito net covering is fine. So is a wide-mouthed jar with netting or screening over the top. Some people make special caterpillar cages with screened sides and a door. Others put their caterpillars on the food tree and cover the branch with a bag of netting, which they tie at the bottom.

No matter where you keep your caterpillars, remember that their cage should be ventilated. They need clean fresh air. Caterpillars do better, too, when kept in the shade and not in direct sunlight.

When you find a caterpillar, remember what kind of leaves it was eating and keep on feeding that kind to it. Chances are it will refuse to eat anything else. The leaves must be fresh and should usually be changed every day, sometimes oftener. The leaves can be kept fresh for longer periods of time by placing the branch in a small glass jar filled with water. But be sure to stuff the opening with cotton or paper, so that the caterpillar doesn't fall in and drown.

Keep the caterpillar cage clean by removing all droppings and wilted foliage every day. If any caterpillar becomes sick or diseased, remove it at once so that its companions won't be infected. With good care your caterpillars should flourish. You can watch them spin cocoons or transform into chrysalises. Best of all, you can see the adult butterflies and moths when they emerge.

When a caterpillar is ready to pupate, it stops eating and empties waste material from its body. Sometimes it changes color. It often becomes restless and wanders about looking for a good place to transform into the pupal, or resting, stage.

*The Butterfly Chrysalis*

A butterfly caterpillar does not spin a cocoon. Instead it transforms into a particular kind of pupa that is called a chrysalis. When it finds a suitable spot, the butterfly caterpillar spins a silken pad, which it hangs onto with its hind prolegs. Some, such as the monarch caterpillar, hang head down-

The monarch caterpillar hangs upside down
when it transforms into a chrysalis.

ward. Others, such as swallowtail caterpillars, remain right side up, for they have also spun a silken loop that supports them around the middle. They hang against it as a window washer high on a building hangs against his straps.

Whichever way it hangs, the caterpillar remains motionless for some hours. At last it sheds its skin once more. Now it is a chrysalis.

Chrysalises are hard to find outdoors, for they are usually hidden in out-of-the-way places. They have many strange shapes and often look like bits of bark or dead leaves. A few of them are ornamented with gold or silver spots.

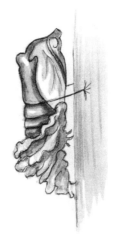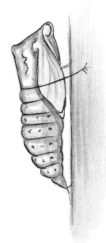

The tiger swallowtail caterpillar spins a silken loop and hangs against it.

Some moth caterpillars burrow into the ground when they are ready to pupate. The huge hickory horned devil does this. So do many others, including the horned caterpillars of sphinx moths. Others crawl into crevices of bark or under stones and old logs. They often pupate without spinning cocoons.

*Spinning a Cocoon*

Most moth caterpillars, however, spin cocoons about themselves before they become pupae. It is very interesting to watch them doing this.

A big Cecropia caterpillar starts its cocoon by coating a twig with silk. Its head moves busily back and forth as the spinneret leaves a fine silk thread on everything it touches. The silk comes out of the spinneret as a liquid, which immediately hardens into gleaming thread.

Gradually the Cecropia caterpillar fashions a silken net about itself. Working tirelessly it fills in the empty spaces. At last a big bag takes shape.

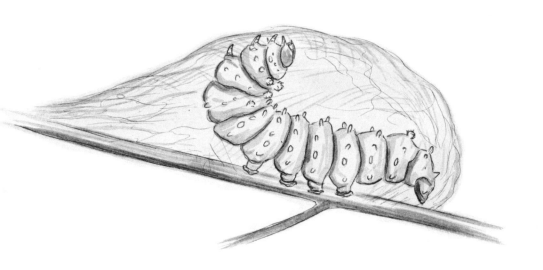

You can still see the caterpillar through the thin walls. But gradually, as it adds layer after layer of silk, the caterpillar conceals itself inside the cocoon.

After the outside wall is finished, the Cecropia caterpillar spins a second oval-shaped cocoon inside the large bag. This gives added protection against enemies and weather.

The Polyphemus caterpillar spins an oval white cocoon with just one wall. When it has finished spinning, it discharges a liquid that soaks into the silk and hardens like cement. The Polyphemus cocoon is tough and waterproof.

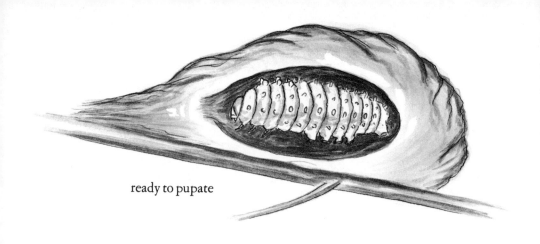

ready to pupate

When its cocoon is completed, the moth caterpillar rests quietly inside its prison of silk. If you
carefully cut a window in the newly made cocoon
with a pair of nail scissors, you can watch what
happens next.

### The Moth Pupa

For several days the caterpillar shrivels and
shrinks. It looks as if it is dying. But it is just getting ready to shed its skin one more time. Finally
the skin splits down the back and is cast off behind.
The caterpillar has transformed into a pale, soft pupa.

The pupa quickly hardens and becomes dark
brown. It looks like a little mummy case. *Pupa* is a

Latin word that means *doll* or *puppet.* The pupa cannot walk. But it can wriggle. The pupa of the luna moth is especially lively. It twists and turns, making the thin-walled cocoon move about.

A moth pupa looks very different from the caterpillar it once was. The caterpillar prolegs have disappeared, and on the outside of the pupa you can trace the outline of the different parts of the adult moth. The wings show as little pads. Between them are the feathery moth antennae and the legs, all folded together.

Great changes take place inside the pupa, too. All the internal organs of the caterpillar quickly dissolve, and the pupa at first seems to be filled

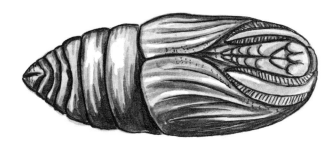

The pupa looks like a mummy case.

Polyphemus cocoon

with a milky liquid. Gradually the organs of the moth form around special clusters of cells, or tissue buds. We still do not know exactly how this happens.

*Cocoon Hunting*

Besides raising caterpillars and watching them spin cocoons, you can also hunt for cocoons. The best time is fall and winter, when trees are bare.

Your eyes become sharp at spotting the big baggy cocoons of Cecropias and the smaller oval cocoons

60

Promethea cocoons

of Polyphemus moths. The cocoon of the Promethea moth is a bit harder to recognize. It looks like a dried leaf hanging to a branch. Luna-moth cocoons are even more difficult to find. Spun among leaves, they usually lie hidden on the ground.

Don't keep your cocoons in the house. The heat will make them hatch during the winter. An unheated porch or garage is the best place for them. There the cocoons will hatch at the normal time. If the air is very dry, you can occasionally sprinkle them with a little water.

It is very exciting to watch a butterfly emerge from its chrysalis, or a moth from its cocoon. You can sometimes see the butterfly's colored wings through the walls of the chrysalis and tell when it is getting ready to hatch. Then, if you keep a close check, you may see the butterfly split the shell of the chrysalis and scramble out.

You will usually have no way of knowing, however, just when a moth cocoon is going to hatch. If you are lucky, you may see a wet stain at the end of the cocoon. It means that the moth is struggling free of the pupal case and has discharged a liquid to soften the silk fibers of the cocoon. It is getting ready to break through and emerge. Sometimes you can even hear it as it struggles to come out.

monarch butterfly emerging from its chrysalis

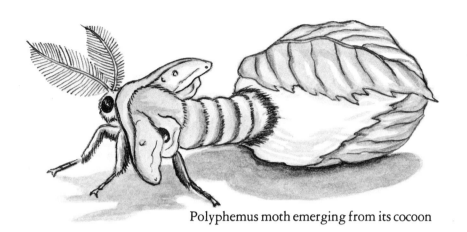

Polyphemus moth emerging from its cocoon

*A Moth Emerges*

What a strange-looking creature a big moth is as it hatches from the cocoon. First come the head and legs, and the huge feathery antennae. Legs waving wildly, the moth pulls its wings out, and then its soft body. Free of the cocoon, it scrambles about until it finds a good resting place. Then it hangs quietly. The long body is wet and bedraggled, and the wings are tiny little pads no bigger than your thumbnails.

But watch carefully. The wings gradually become larger and larger as the moth pumps blood through the tubes that form the framework of the wings. In about half an hour the wings reach full size. But they are still damp, and soft as cloth. It will take several hours for them to stiffen and dry.

The moth does not fly, however, until night comes. As darkness falls, it spreads its lovely wings. For a moment the wings tremble, then they begin to flap. Finally the moth takes off and flutters away.

Somewhere in the night it will find a mate. Then the female moth will lay her eggs. Soon tiny caterpillars will start the cycle all over again.